# Praise for *A Playbill for Sunset*

"When you encounter a poem by Dan Campion—and they have been appearing all over the place for many years now—you know you are going to be surprised by rhyme and entranced by smart formal choices. In this amazing book of (mostly) sonnets, Campion demonstrates some of the wild surprises that long-tested form still holds, in skilled hands like his. Poem after poem, you find yourself possessed for a moment, maybe by laughter or tears or something else hard to name—some complex possession of loss that arrives only after you have lost what you thought you possessed."
—Ed Folsom, Roy J. Carver Professor of English and Director, Undergraduate Creative Writing Program, University of Iowa

"In *A Playbill for Sunset*, Dan Campion meditates, like Montaigne, on a vast array of subjects—cicadas, the iridium layer of Earth, a Seurat painting, the tarantella—but most of all on time, and the way it both flies and freezes. Each poem is intelligent, questing, elegantly rhymed and metered, in various forms, but with more sonnets than anything else. These restrained, elegiac poems cast an unhurried and appreciative gaze on everything from the sparrows in a hedge to a spray-painted old car, abandoned and corroding in the woods. Anything, looked at reflectively, can contain worlds."
—Susan McLean, author of *The Best Disguise* (winner of the Richard Wilbur Award) and *The Whetstone Misses the Knife* (winner of the Donald Justice Poetry Prize)

"The weight of life, of wisdom won through grief and loss, through attention paid to experience, all show in these fine poems, a master's class in formal structures and the art of finding new turns of thought summoned by their rigors." — David Hamilton, author of A Certain Arc: Essays of *Finding My Way* and *Ossabaw: Poem* and longtime editor of *The Iowa Review*

# A Playbill for Sunset

## Dan Campion

Ice Cube Press, LLC (Est. 1991)
North Liberty, Iowa, USA

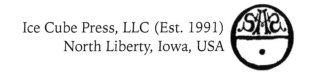

Cover illustration: Astrid Hilger Bennett, *Dreaming Quilt #5:
Summer Light 2*

Author portrait by Joseph Patrick

For JoAnn

# Contents

# A Playbill for Sunset

# Time's Arrow

We're not in any rush. Time goes both ways.
Our toes turn into heels and heels to toes.
Some spin their wheels, do donuts, catch the craze
their screens display. Not us. We're through with those.
Time's so much better now, its arrowhead
as soft as feathers, and its feathers flint,
by turns. For decades we had thought it sped
just one way. That was one disastrous stint.
The field is open, cleared of stubble, disced
and plowed and ready for new planting. Who
recalls the deep time and steep odds we risked?
The arrow shaft dissolved as archer drew.
Thoreau could find an arrowhead and hear
the breathing of the hunter and the deer.

# New Year's Morning

A flock of sparrows find a hedge and make
it theirs for warmth and camouflage and shade.
They never plant a flag or drive a stake.
I've yet to see a rival mount a raid;
the hawks and crows and owls can't get in there,
and other flocks of sparrows don't invade.
Although Utopias of twigs are spare,
I doubt a sounder plan was ever made.
Inside, the sparrows chatter favorite lines
from *Hamlet* and the King James Version, not
the lines you'd think, but melody that twines
among the words, a pagan polyglot.
The tiny prince and choir are at it now
beneath the snow that covers every bough.

# St. Mary's

When Flannery O'Connor sat in church
she sometimes thought about the captive bear
across the river in his little cage
inside the kiddie zoo in City Park.
His being there where children stopped to stare
in mirth or pity must fill out a page
that needed filling. Still, one had to search
for words. To cast their beams into the dark.
The proper angle, always hard to gauge,
one hair's breadth off was certain to besmirch
a certainty essential to the care
of every soul. You had to mind each mark.
A comma out of place might damn this town.
Grant mercy, she thought, eyeing Mary's crown.

# The Slate-Colored Junco

Gray sky and frozen ground, the junco pecked
and pecked at frozen grass between stone slabs
and at the slabs themselves. You would expect
futility to look like vacant jabs,
but when the junco fluttered to the hedge
its flight was sure and purposeful, as if
its cold and empty feast fulfilled a pledge,
revisited a scene, reprised a riff.
You can't retrace the scrollwork of such acts,
just indicate them with a look or nod.
The more details, the more each one detracts,
until the liveliest descriptions plod.
We'll leave the junco in the hedge, one stroke
of slate gray placed there just as morning broke.

# Das Boot

My claustrophobia prevented me
from entering the submarine, although
its trundling through Chicago's streets would be
my first dada/surrealism show;
to get the U-boat to its final berth
at the museum through the city grid,
the moving crew unhinged the steady earth
as surely as Duchamp and Breton did.
Das Boot was thus complicit in the change
from war to wonder. Nothing was the same
past nineteen fifty-four, whose making-strange
spread wild as prairie grasses set aflame
yet chilled the flesh like cold Atlantic waves,
a Proteus who freezes whom he saves.

# The Interpreter

When Lincoln picked up *Leaves of Grass* and read
aloud, his colleagues paused. Their legal chores
could wait. To hear, through him, what Whitman said
was something special. One thought Walt a bore,
another, dangerous; opinions veered.
But now, in Lincoln's voice, "I celebrate
myself" came naturally forth fresh and clear.
"The distillation would intoxicate
me also, but I shall not let it"; plain
air bests perfumes? Well, that makes sense enough
in Springfield, where verbena traced the lanes.
It compensates for lines that came out rough.
And even those, he gave an etiquette
his partner and his clerk would not forget.

# Hild

The top floor of the factory was all mine
to manage: bins of motors, castings, gears
and screws and bearings, destined for the line
where they'd be mingled as floor polishers.
The pigeons roosting there at night would coo
at six a.m. and exit through the frame
a broken window left behind. A few
assemblers might shag parts at them—their aim
was never true—then hand me paper slips
some supervisor'd scrawled on, "six spray hoods
& 24 steel clamps," and I'd make trips
by dicey elevator with the goods.
To stop, you yanked a frayed rope in the shaft,
and, hit the basement hard, the lathe guys laughed.

# Ferlinghetti

When I barged in his office door
Admitting North Beach traffic's roar,
A stranger from the Middle West
In beard and jeans and rawhide vest,
He might have simply said, "So long,"
And who'd have thought him in the wrong?
Instead, he gave me such a look
As you might guess who've read the book
I held out, nerves in disarray,
Forgetting what I'd meant to say,
My heart in Tilt-a-Whirl dismay,
And with a smile both beat and kind
Dear Lawrence Ferlinghetti signed
*A Coney Island of the Mind.*

# The Greystone

Some archaeologists are digging bricks
from sand and clay right now. They excavate
as long as budget holds, and politics
and sun and tides and wind cooperate.
They'll build an image up, from what they find,
of structures and their use. They'll populate
whole towns, learn how they prayed and worked and dined,
and, daring censure, may extrapolate.
My aims are narrower. On Fremont Street
the greystone where you lived still stands, its blocks
of limestone lodged in place, a frozen fleet,
inside them, trade in words no spell unlocks.
Perhaps when fallen, washed away, dissolved,
they'll yield the terms on which our lives revolved.

# The Parrots

We're colorful. We wear our epaulettes
with pride and toss our heads back to recite,
our feathers better fit for show than flight.
We're doormen who imagine they're cadets.
We were the ones who didn't see the nets,
got tangled up in them, and sick with fright
were shipped here to give service and delight.
Salons on better streets keep us as pets.
We give them back their words, but with a bite
of the exotic, like a taste of lime
or ginger, and a twang shaped by the beak.
It's marvelous how we clutch, over time,
a perch so slick, so worn, so hard, so slight.
Flung to the gutter, even there we're chic.

# Belle Epoque

A tree removed down to the roots may leave
a circle twenty years or more in grass.
The soil remembers, though it cannot grieve,
the shadows' green processions as they pass.
A fountain's mist can hover in the air
forever in a green, receptive mind
attracted by a momentary flare
of sun as water jets rise close-entwined.
Give over melancholy. When Satie
arrives, receive him in a cheerful mood,
steep for you both a pot of English tea,
refuse all evening long the urge to brood.
Observe the ironwork's entangled vines
and scrolls while strolling home to pen your lines.

# Neap Tide

We waded in a tide of words, then dove
headfirst and swam out far as we'd been taught
was safe, then turned to our protected cove
and, seeing sand where ancient armies fought,
grasped where we were and how we had been schooled,
and turned again, and strove amid blue waves
and glaucous swells, hearts set not to be ruled
by lessons hatched in mansions that held slaves.
Their towers and their widow's walks we saw
from far out, taking one look back before
we plunged toward open ocean, lungs now raw
from heavy work that bore us far from shore.
We're creatures, now, of currents, where we drift
amid lost masts and wheels that dip and lift.

# Little Victories

Invidious comparison is all
that makes a little victory small. *Don't make
me laugh,* you're bound to counter. *Small is small.*
To which I'll say: But you're forgetting Blake.
You know, his universal grain of sand,
his endless hour. *He knew,* you'll say, *for us
to see the spirit flea, it must expand.
A tiny ghost would look ridiculous.*
Then I'd insist a victory's not a flea,
and naturally our talk would fall apart;
but you'd applaud me on my victory.
The sound of one hand clapping is grand art.
Once more I've pierced the needle with a thread
I moistened with a lick mere fancy bred.

# The Tarantella

Some claim the tarantella is a dance
to cure a spider's bite, while others say
it is no "dance" but just the way we prance
and gambol when the spider's had her way
with us and made us puppets on her thread.
I'm neutral in this great debate. The notes
can be read either way, I think, as bred
to play on poisons or their antidotes.
You'll have to make your own mind up: bite, cure,
both, neither, or some fifth alternative
we can't imagine though our hearts are pure
and logic flawless. Which view would you give?
The likelihood is that you won't be tasked
to say. But are you ready, if you're asked?

# A View Over the Bay

At last we're not constrained by anything,
dissolving back into the larger world,
one atom to a bow, one to a string,
one to a fiddlehead fern tightly curled.
Confined to stone, some trace of us is just
a listener on a different scale of time,
who hears the mountains grind away to dust
and notices the glaciers speak in rhyme.
The greater part of us disperses wide.
Deep space, deep time do not begin to say
how far. There are more tides beyond the tide
of our affairs in this sequestered bay.
Our maps and charts diffuse as well, reclaimed
to swell the very lands and seas they named.

# Proof of Concept

Our mountainless horizon trains the eye
to recognize in plane geometry
the hunched leviathan that $x$ and $y$
do not describe. Let right triangles be
the flukes and semicircles serve as ribs.
Each great eye narrows to a single point.
Then proofs and lemmas are so many squibs
we scrape across the slate, their strokes disjoint
as ancient corals left by vanished seas
new rivulets expose to April rains,
whose scribbles in soft stone wear by degrees
to powder. No one's tallying up gains.
The sun drags out its single evening chore,
to sweep up litter off the trading floor.

# Bloodroot

Descending the steep path one April dusk
I saw the old oak fallen on its side.
The clay socket, the bark, were dry husk.
Elephantine branches arrayed death wide
as an ashen century oak can spread.
The tree, standing the winter to fall in spring
beneath an eastward-driving thunderhead,
loomed in its own shade now in the quiet clearing.
Along the low hill that received the shock
of the fall, rows of small white blossoms close
at sunset, each one cowled in the reeding
of a single fresh green leaf.  They are a flock,
unagitated by the tree's repose,
their red roots live, fibrous, and unbleeding.

# The Iridium Layer

We'll note, to start, its thinness—hardly there—
and next, the chalky pallor of the layer.
Your eyes will want to wander high and low,
comparing depths. Don't let them. Let the glow
of the iridium command your gaze,
just as its meteor set skies ablaze.
Now test the rock for friability
by scraping with your penknife. Soon you'll see
how fragile even earthshakers can be,
gods ground up in their own catastrophe.
Already, now, you're on your own. You don't
need me. Go on to smell and taste. You won't?
You say you can't, would rather not? Well, then.
We'll wait here till the sky burns up again.

# The Great Pyramid of Des Moines

I love your planes and spaces, I. M. Pei,
but why do you never drain the rain away?
Right in front of Roy Lichtenstein's *Great
Pyramid*, your roof has made a little lake.
Why doesn't the American Institute of Arts and Letters
care that in Boston your windows are falling on pedestrians?
In Sarasota the college you raised
is sinking back into the Everglades.
I hear the same thing wherever I go:
The man's a genius, but – *Look out below*.
Yet all your buildings win the big awards:
I guess this reconfirms that "Less is more."
Since you're making icons of our age,
of course they run, crack, chip, peel, split, and fade.

# The Rental

The backyard was a cup formed by low hills
where fireflies would glint and swirl like snow
and snow like galaxies. Such light distills
a place, lets you forget what you don't know:
the first inhabitants, if they had time
to watch the spectacles or even cared,
who built the house, who lived there in its prime,
what banister came loose but got repaired,
how many rafters, studs, and laths kept things
together, what fasteners it took,
how many vibrant particles or strings
made up the pale blue beadboard kitchen nook.
From seven years' familiarity
we took our leave immersed in mystery.

# Diving

The boys would disappear beneath the bridge
and, current flowing south, they'd reappear
some twenty yards downstream, by boathouse ridge.
The younger boys upstream sent down a cheer.
However, it was their turn now to leap
from second-story height through river's blaze
of ripples, plunging down but not so deep
they'd strike the bottom lost in weedy haze.
We crossed to reach the public swimming pool
a half mile to the north, where lifeguards reigned
and placards spelled out every rigid rule.
We heard sharp splashes, saw green shoreline gained,
looked forward to our swim in roped-off lane
while from the bridge boys dived and dived again.

# In Elburn, Illinois

We stopped to see Dave Etter, knowing him
just from his poems. Of course he didn't know
us. You weren't happy, as your view was dim
of dropping in. You thought it didn't show
respect. But Mr. Etter served us tea
and didn't seem the least put out. You'd think
he'd been expecting us. His poetry
drew people in; you met them with a drink
appropriate to age and hour, and spoke
commensurately. I think this must have been,
now, forty years ago, enough to stoke
a fire to get the train to Galveston.
The years burn up like dry wood. This, Dave knew,
took time for us, and let the tea slow-brew.

# Tornado Sonnet

Forewarned, we crouch beneath the cellar stair.
The howl starts low ("I saw the best minds . . .")
then zooms Lear-ward and scales up from there,
climbing where *Fidelio* unwinds.
Cannonballs start hammering the roof—
Are we the *Monitor* or *Merrimac*?—
Van Allen belts set flailing offer proof
spacetime itself is bent to the attack.
Abandoned by all useful thought, we clutch
each other, plunged in sudden silent dark
amid a Dantesque jumble; here's a crutch,
and there's an oar, to stave off Charon's barque.
The all-clear sounds. School out from shadowed cave,
we scan our town to see what we can save.

# Late May

Today the leaves begin their summer loll
and toss. They've just begun to do that thing
that makes you think of water rippling
and renders winter's frigid limbs banal.
They answer to the tutelage of Sol,
the constellations' hectoring through spring,
and sweetness from gorged sapwood's watering,
all echoes of old folk songs' folderol.
They make an old man edgy and obtuse.
He feels the languor in the green display,
and hears susurrus clearly, likes the shade,
but can't unsee the leaves falling away
and heartwood cut and put to vulgar use:
any use that answers to a blade.

# Episode

Once my wife stood at the kitchen door
observing a yellow-shafted flicker
sifting through our lawn, when a
redtail hit the smaller hunger and bore
it away toward the hickory grove.

Today, a feather drifting by my window
sends me a fuzzy touch screen shot:
some talons' daily quota has been met.
A bubble of air distressed in the glass
glows like the dot of an antique TV set.

The evidence is the mystery:
sand embracing leaves and bark,
swimmerets, weaving, cast in rock,
gleaners, stooped by sack or creel,
scraping at tides to scrounge a meal.

Where artery begets vein, stories begin.
Each episode's the molting of a skin,
the curl of a cloud, the dip of a wing
no one sees and when they hear of it
do not know for precisely what it is.

Precisely what it is is the whole story.
As leafsquall gambles the daylight away
its tent is a temporary cathedral
ancient as the untrustworthy arch
of a soaring raptor's prim dihedral.

# Green

This morning dawned that green that's frightening,
by sign, not of tornado weaving near,
but of green shade, green fuse, that likening
of mood to boundless growth, like unchecked fear.
The air feels close as under greenhouse glass,
smells rank with pollen, creek bed mud, sour seeds,
and glazes careless eye like ditch weed grass.
It whispers we're not what this landscape needs.
It wants to cover us, root through our bones
toward soil more nurturing. It wants to jade
and emerald its way past whites and browns
to rule by clover leaf and saw grass blade.
Terroir, that vintner's term, describes the reign
of water over blood in green's domain.

# The Inchworm

A spot of green against a scrim of leaves,
the inchworm, hanging by a thread of sun,
is easy prey. A swallow as it weaves
nearby ignores it. I'm the only one,
it seems, who notices the tiny stir
the inchworm makes while dangling in still air.
I can't help thinking, though, it won't endure
for long. I'll blink and it will not be there.
Or it will blink and I'll be gone instead.
Do inchworms have eyes? Eyelids that can shut?
Perhaps we're both inside each other's head,
each, spider to the other, quick to cut
or spin another thread, as might be best,
to fetch a find back home, or clean the nest.

# Tomato Vines

We cage them now. They used to be staked out,
tied up with old dishrag or T-shirt strip
to lumber scrap, as soon as first green sprout
and flower showed which way the fruit would tip.
The stem, as prickly as a boar's-hair brush,
might scrape the fingers that would tie the knot,
and certainly perfumed them with a lush
bouquet of mint and grass and compost rot.
The clusters hidden in among the leaves,
when brought to light, might wear a strangled look,
garrotted by the knotted rag that weaves
from packet seeds to garden plot to cook.
We'd pick the red, ripe fruit and leave the rest,
and loose or cinch the knot as we thought best.

# Woods

They drove a '68 Electra deep
inside the woods and left it there. When I
first saw it, it stood on its roof, a heap
stripped of its tires, already sunk trunk-high
in spongy earth and undergrowth, and bright
with polychrome Day-Glo graffiti.
It made a cheerful sculpture in the light
that filtered through the old-growth canopy.
Some flood years and some drought years on, the car
has settled to a hulk of rust that might
evoke a baby mammoth stuck in tar.
You wouldn't want to come out here at night,
get haunted by machines the forest gnaws,
the locomotives, ships, planes, snarled chain saws.

# Found Object

*After an anonymous work*

A flourish of graffiti wreathes the wreck
upended on its roof where river trail
bends tight as horseshoe, limp as broken neck,
around the stand of trash trees in the vale.
This isn't gallery work put up for sale,
no sign of empire rotting in the wood,
it's just a car some kids headed for jail
took spray cans to, from fins to ripped-off hood.
It makes you look around, for your own good,
to see who might be lurking in the brush.
"Outsider art" museumed sets a mood,
but in the field like this, you get a rush.
I doubt this car gets dragged back to the road.
We leave it here in splendor to corrode.

# Practically Speaking

There's actually a red wheelbarrow in
our neighbor's yard. He's out there now, spade clasped
in hand. The wheelbarrow, though, has been
perched on a stump, its right arm cleanly snapped
off at the shoulder, for a month or so,
and upside down of course to keep rain out.
Don't want to see mosquito numbers grow.
He'll fix it, though. His gardening's devout.
The silver maple that rose from the stump,
a hundred-year tree, shaded half the plot
and had to go. He's hoeing at a clump
of chard. Perhaps the tree was showing rot.
I haven't got the heart to question him
about it, or the barrow's missing limb.

# Les Îles de la Grande Jatte

*after Seurat's* A Sunday on La Grande Jatte—1884

Park crews arranged the seedlings long ago.
I bring the Sunday crowd and pose them more
or less correctly on the lawn. They go
about their business as they've done before,
a flick of ash, a squint at farther shore.
They humor me, refrain from pointing out
where I've misplaced a boat or character.
My memory is imperfect, without doubt.
I'm struck by their civility: no shout
of greeting, nor a sign of any kind.
Their faith in my discretion is devout
despite my faults. The best friends one could find.
Two canopies of green spread overhead.
My butterfly is orange and black, theirs, red.

# Cottonmouth

There is no mystery when the fangs go in.
Of course a different thing, uncertainty,
arises when a cottonmouth strikes. Skin
deep? Deeper? Venom dose: full potency?
What volume was injected? Who can say?
It happened quickly, though time seemed to slow.
The nearest doctor's three hours' hike away.
Has he got antivenin? We don't know.
We're shackled to the situation tight
as slaves to oars, chain gangs to iron rings.
The cottonmouth is curled up for the night,
already buried in replenishing
its store of poison, languidly, asleep
almost, more coiled-up lashes in its keep.

# Out Back

The furrowed acre out back,
a back badly scarred,
is gone to weeds
and tanned tops of seeds
of whatever was supposed to grow
out back. The season bleeds away
through cracking fence rails toward the highway.
The highway leads through DeKalb corn signs
to the mountains. Frank reads the papers and takes
an occasional drink. Charles teaches and tries not to think
of a silver crane against the blue, wings spread like a golden field.
We are all coasting. Across the scene, flushed from the swaying limbs
of the windbreak, redwings blow like hats, abandoning
the silver poplars to a breeze. No one believes
he has seen his life before. Skittering across
the surface of the creek, arrow-headed
insects tend the stream, beneath which
rocks grow backwards into
green and ochre grains.
Soon smoke will rise
from piled leaves, boys
staring into their flames.

# Monarchy

We wouldn't say the monarch butterfly
had sinned or made an error when it fixed
on milkweed as its sine qua non. Why
is obvious. However much we've mixed
ourselves up, we do not presume to judge
the monarchs. Nor, presumably, do they
judge us, though virgin land reduced to drudge
looks like our doing. We will fade away
like former plagues, droughts, glaciers, floods, and fires.
The only questions are, How soon? In time?
but why should they arise since what transpires
is unaffected by surmise? We rhyme
with previous misfortunes. Unjust kings
all fall at last beneath fierce beating wings.

# The Inlet

It's morning, speedboats nibbling the far edge
of watery light. This side, lunkers rise
like Zeppelins through their cloud-embellished sky
to crop the algae off crazed glacial stones.
As yet, no snakes are sunning on the rocks
above the shore; one guards his burrow door.
I turn and walk the trail, repeating names
aloud where nothing but the forest hears.
No echo can return, each sound absorbed
by broad leaves, needles, feathers, petals, burrs,
the soil itself that sinks down toward the lake.
There is no path here thinking fears to take.
The last act of the last mind at the last:
to watch the flickers build their nest in shade.

## Peace Garden

Hand me the garden spade and hoe and rake
if you can find them in the cluttered shed.
Fetch me the sacks of mulch, the string to stake,
the can for watering, the seed to spread.
Then lead me, like those boys who had no masks,
or did not don them fast enough, who won
the war but lost their sight, to where my tasks
begin to end all wars. Sufficient sun,
manure, and rain may not be forthcoming.
There is no fence. The weevil and the wren
will claim their shares before the harvesting,
and slugs and greedy mice and hungry men.
I cannot see the way. But lead me there
to tend the soil and breathe the morning air.

# The Sublime

*for David Yerkes*

Afield in storms, Douglas tempted lightning.
Jim hit frostbite like black ice on slick roads.
I've swayed on ledges wearying to climb.
But you, David, ranged the manifold modes
Of the sublime.
                           Rushes of prairie grass
Are weaving in that clearing by the dam.
The creek's alive with crawfish and darters.
This spring the wild geraniums bloomed late
But lasted into May, almost to June.
The woods you memorized
                           rethink themselves.
The smallest movement of the brush will change
The portrait of a forest. That's mere art.
Your use of bark as snare and armature
To catch an anxious mind and hold it fast
Is more than artifice can do.
                           To know
The trails at night or drifted deep with snow,
To feel the roots beneath your shoes connect
To leaflets in the crowns of ash and oak,
To sense the Canadas before they swoop
Full-throated just above the canopy,
Is not to paint the woods,
                           but be them.
This copse at the crest of Hickory Hill
Draws trails, roads, and flyways together.
I come here for our conversations' sake,
Those models of reciprocal soundings,
Forgetting I can tell you nothing new
Now you're at one with everything in view.
You've become the elder, and I keep still,
Attentive to each hint in these surroundings.

# The Fawn

The doe arrives with one fawn, one too few.
They crop the grass as usual. The doe's
ribs look too visible. The whole world knows
what's happening, but I just wish I knew,
while at the same time turning down each clue.
It doesn't matter. Grass when cropped regrows,
replenished by hard rain, the dry creek flows.
Those absent still possess the breath they drew.
The smoke of fires upwind grays up the sky.
The fawn looks fireward, startled, leaps, and flees,
her mother following, then in the lead,
both sheltering among obscurities,
both blending into landscape as they fly
from sight behind the scrim of brush and reed.

# The Hounds

We also glimpsed the goddess. When she saw
our master, her excitement swept the glade.
Actaeon soon lay rent by tooth and claw
completely shorn as if by Hector's blade.
Whose punishment was harsher, his or ours?
We had to watch our lord's flesh come apart
just like a stag's, though easier by far,
among us, raw, untouched as yet by art.
There wasn't anything our pack could do
to heal his wounds and raise him up again.
All blamed Diana, but it wasn't true.
Kept dogs act on their own not if, but when.
His people came and took him. We stayed here,
thick woods gone dark but our eyes grey and clear.

# The Lyrebird

*Surely one of the most extraordinary voices in the animal kingdom.*—Jennifer Ackerman in The Bird Way

Adept in mimicry, the lyrebird
can sound like almost anything: ax blows,
a banjo's twang, a cello's highs and lows,
and scores of different birds. It seems absurd,
so deep a repertoire in just one bird,
and why it's so prolific no one knows.
Oh, there are theories, couched in careful prose,
but none would dare to claim the final word.
I think the lyrebird gives prose the lie
by telling lies that tell the truth, in verse,
net up, in imitation of the leaves,
the waves, the raptor's cry, the quarry's curse.
But lyrebird, too, may deceive. Truths fly
at speeds no swooping peregrine achieves.

# Folktale

The sawyer cut a log in twain lengthwise,
and out of one half stepped a comely lad,
an ogre from the other. No surprise,
the sawyer grumbled. All my luck runs bad.
The sawyer's daughter, at her window, sad
as usual, was overjoyed to see
two new companions. One looked slightly mad.
The other, though, looked handsome as could be;
she thought like lightning, He's the one for me!
She meant the ogre, naturally. He snared
her heart by means that stayed a mystery
to sawyer, comely lad, and dam. They dared
not ask. Some things are better left to guess,
and halving logs proves often profitless.

# The Frog Prince

The prince, when he became a prince again,
so horrified the frogs that they began
a chant of mourning, not for what he'd been,
but for the monster he'd become: a man.
Once lovely green, with one leap he could span
the pond, and in a flicker catch a fly.
His metamorphosed shape had no clear plan,
a pale leviathan. They'd sooner die
than take that goblin shape, cast that strange eye
across the lilies and the lotus blooms
from such a distance he could not descry
his friends, his rightful clan, his sumptuous rooms.
A prince, they sputtered, what is that? A curse
which they could find no Merlin to reverse.

# Repertoires

Invisible, but frenzied in their cries,
some barred owls congregating in the woods
are casting spells. As pitch and volume rise
they do *Macbeth*'s three witches. Neighborhoods
for miles may hear their variations on
"Young Goodman Brown." They're pleased to share
assorted takes from the *Decameron*
and chants I've never heard from who knows where.
Wagnerian, I almost want to say,
but saying anything would seem to miss
the point. For all of that, I scratch away,
in words on paper, lines that crawl and hiss:
three quatrains and a couplet, past midnight
and muted by their muses' silent flight.

# The Armadillo

This one we can't run over
nor sell its hide in stores
like other armadillos'
with lesser armorers.

We can't divine its gender
nor color deep inside
the plates of sturdy chitin,
which can't be pierced or pried.

This one fulfills the daydream
of children of all kinds
that they might wear a garment
as steely as their minds.

We will not solve its mystery
until the creature dies.
But it should live forever,
just judging by its eyes.

# Stridulation

Strident, strident, strident, all day long
the fields and trees alive with locusts fleer
at every semblance of a human song.
If any of us sang, no one would hear.
The mockery's infernal. Crawled from earth
and climbed up every stem and stalk and spire
of bark, the little gargoyles vent their mirth
like fumaroles, the netherworld's own choir.
My neighbors told me they don't mind the din.
They said it tells them nature carries on
in spite of us. At that I stepped back in
my house and shut the windows, patience gone.
Chamomile won't always calm a night.
Fresh stridulation strikes up at first light.

# Corn Moon, Daylight

September's full night moon just one day past,
its ghost fades into pale blue toward the west
with softened edges and a Grant Wood cast,
that shade of laundered chintz with which he dressed
his subjects, clinging still like maizy silk
to rolling hills and farmer's daughter's gaze.
Look again: a pail of watery milk
seen from the loft, the ghost moon steeps in haze.
Then goes, bleached into flat horizon line,
beyond retouching by the soft dry brush
of "corn moon" country. Elsewhere it may shine
with brilliance in a more respectful hush.
Not that the moon relies on our say-so
to paint its face or make tides ebb and flow.

# Dispositions

The furniture gets moved around, a spouse
discloses hidden parts, your neighborhood
bleeds into other neighborhoods, the house
decides it isn't brick or stone or wood
or even glass, but light spread on a lawn
of uncut grass, of crisping leaves, of snow.
As soon as you see what it is, it's gone,
including contents you'd professed to know.
A claim of knowledge holds high standing here
the better to be toppled, charred, and spread
out thin, a burnt note in the atmosphere.
Most voices we recall, not what they said,
which probably was neither here nor there,
stray senses blent like ashes into air.

# Out on Route 6

It's not a churchyard,
but everything's decent, naturally.
A few spruces and spreading pines,
lawn well tended,
unobstructed view of the countryside.
Hardly a traveler's oasis,
but you could do worse
for accommodations.
I've got no business here,
but sometimes you ought to
stop for strangers
and make an effort at least
to puzzle out their oldest names.
This local stone is soft,
so the long ancestral eulogies are lost.
The deepest words have wept,
like dripping paint,
but some remain.
Cherry / Eighteen sixty-three /
These grew like trees /
Plum / Eighteen fifty-six /
blossomed, and went to seed.
There are new granite markers
with open dates,
harder still to read.
The fields around
are ready for winter.
Nevertheless, this crisp afternoon
has brought out a horse and rider
cantering with a dog a mile away,
framed against the sky by evergreens,
and the sun stirs some brittle
cicadas for a few hours of Indian summer.
Here, listening, stands a living monument,

gauging the hue of the red-cedar berries,
studying a curious medallion that proves
to be a spider astride the last dandelion,
learning the chill of sun
on seared stone, each finally
strange as a fresh-fallen meteor.

# Stranded

The castaways on islands share one hope,
to spy a sail and catch a lookout's eye.
Without such fantasies, they'd scarcely cope
with their predicament, and cease to try,
with those crude tools they've fashioned, to survive.
We understand this in our DNA,
from which we can't escape, while we're alive,
but hope we may transcend come Judgment Day,
which day is differently defined on Crete,
Manhattan, Pago Pago, and Timor.
We know we're stranded: each feels incomplete,
and with a weather eye patrols the shore,
now gazing far out, now down at our feet.
Feet veined with seaweed, streaked with salt, and sore.

# Uphill on the Plains

The backpackers are practicing once more
here in the lowlands for their mountain trek.
I can't help see their packs as metaphor,
but that's a burden weighing on my neck,
not theirs. They're bound for highlands where the air
thins out, and so will they; light rations slim
you down. Besides, the altitude will pare
away some of this group. They'll reach the rim
of one too many canyons and turn back
or need to be airlifted out. That's just
the way with expeditions. Nerves will crack
and bones may break. The route does as it must.
A storm whips up, we find a rock-faced lee.
The riprap holds until a stone works free.

# The Aspen

A crown of stubborn leaves appears to burn
above its bare and ashen lower limbs.
Once green and silver quaking to each breath
of wind, this poplar's flown to rose and gold.
Suddenly across the clearing comes
its voice. A hundred nimble sparrows send
their matins up, while surpliced neighbor crows
sing vespers. Dawn and dusk now coincide,
as in the August tree's green constellations.
Flat as this unbroken field, the sky
absorbs the susurration of dry leaves.
Those pure, consuming songs it leaves to me.

# Storm Windows

The frame is off, taken to the shop
where new storm windows are made.
Every town has a man in jeans
and a flannel shirt who's better
than you at sealing out the weather.

This spring evening we go to a shower
and admire bibs, crocheted slippers,
and plastic educational toys.
The men take up the hunting season,
the women collect in the kitchen.

Making faces, we inflate balloons
for the children, who wait politely.
As soon as we tie the knots,
the kids elect to break them all.
Outside, a light rain starts to fall.

It doesn't let up till October.
The man in the shop has returned
to Oklahoma. The baby, we heard,
lives with an aunt in Denver.
When will we fix that window?  Never.

# Unfailingly

One day in each October comes an hour
when suddenly, through trees gnawed by the wind,
you hear the trains again. The summer's power
is finally finished when the leaves have thinned.
It isn't that shrill whistles and the grind
of wheels on rails all summer went unheard,
it's just they seldom entered in the mind.
They're different now. They ask to have a word
with you, regardless if you would prefer
or not. They tell you nothing's stopping them.
They own the trestles, town, and sky. You were
in charge, but now you're twisting on a stem,
the cider press is working overtime.
In coming weeks the din can only climb.

# Fom al-Haut

This year, unleafing ash tree's raised one arm
that ends in wave-white ulna pointing south
toward Fomalhaut, in Southern Fish's farm,
that bouillabaisse of churning fin and mouth
and roe where constellations ogle Earth's
equator from their stirred-up wine-dark bowl.
A star's a jaded eye, with many births
and deaths behind its dissipated soul.
So ash tree's handless indicator trues
up on, with kindred stoicism, glint
of glancing recognition as the blues
of evening deepen to the blackest flint
and Fomalhaut, bright star in scaly garb,
takes in the hook of deadwood pointer's barb.

# Wavelength

The difference between oxblood and maroon,
a loden and a Sherwood Forest green,
the tilt of hillside and the switchback swoon
toward gray-brown creek and V of the ravine,
the matter of degree between the tree
that's leafing and the leafless leaned against
it, clinging in last act of ecstasy
before it falls and all this land gets fenced,
as if a single trunk felled silently
or almost silently might be the cue
to end of wilderness, as if one free
or nearly free hour could distinguish blue
of one second of arc of sky from two,
our wavelength tips its gull-wing out of view.

# The Afghans

When winter comes we reach the afghans from
the shelf and spread them on the bed, admire
again their interwoven blue with plum
and sunflower with green. They still inspire
our wonder at the patience they display
and, lacking it, our luck to fall their heir.
The temperature will plummet any day.
We'll wrap ourselves in handmade layer by layer.
You've taken thread and patched them as they aged,
connecting yarns that parted from the strain
of keeping heat in us as we have paged
through Woolf and Whitman, Sappho and Montaigne
while blizzards made their case with blasts and squalls
that piled blank drifts against the clapboard walls.

# The Permanent Crow

sits high up in the winter privet hedge,
asway in breezes, quiet in the calm.
He ducks his head from time to time, on edge,
but doesn't fly his perch, as if some qualm
about the thought of flying kept him there.
Sometimes she raises up her wings and preens
or huddles them the way hawks do to spare
the world the sight of the most bloody scenes.
All winter long it's sat there through the snows
and thaws. The small birds learned ignoring it
incurred no cost to them, and as for crows,
they strut beneath this totem's parapet.
It's grown to look like sere leaves stirred by wind,
a shaggy tale from Poe's pen, plucked and skinned.

# Rime Ice

The fog condensed on every surface clings
and freezes, casting gray and silver nets
on cedars, wrapping oaks in tangled strings
as if a thousand kites had crashed. Ice sets
so quickly, all the kites have turned bone white,
no matter what their vibrant colors were,
and fallen straight, like snow geese shot in flight.
What's under other shapes we can't be sure:
a tangle by the riverside, a hump
beside the trackless path, when spring arrives
we may just see as weeds, a sawed-off stump,
such mundane things as do not touch our lives.
The fog and freeze, though, spread a seine of doubt,
which traps inside us snakes we can't cast out.

# The Scavenger

It's snowing from the ground.
The north wind
peels back seasons,
flails the icy hides, singing

Here are late-month veils,
Here a bloodroot blanket,
Here a morning's clover,
Here the sun's silver ring.

This morning will never end.
The window glass is groaning
to be let in, the doors shake,
the walls shiver, whispering

Snow skirls from the roof,
Ice salts our skin,
Raw from exposure,
And no one is listening.

Blinded and deafened
where the storm wind makes him spin,
amid onerous duties
one crow scrawls with a dipping wing

Here the veil
Here the blanket
Here the clover
Here the ring.

# The Siege

The fortress.
A messenger
glib as heat.

The river.
Bloodroot.
The same river.

Reed baskets,
clay bowls,
wooden spoon.

# The Potter's Wheel

Time is on my hands like slurry clay
from throwing vessels on the potter's wheel.
I'd fetch the pitcher, rinse the film away,
except they say it helps a sore to heal;
I wouldn't know and can't imagine why,
but haven't anything to lose to leave
it coating palms and fingers. Worth a try,
as what is not, when one's inclined to grieve.
Duration is the issue: let it set,
it crabs the grip. Your hands are useless then
as sculpted hands. What compliments they get
won't feed you. There you'll waste, right where you've been.
Perhaps that's what you want to do. Why not?
But first, just one more bowl, vase, dish, cup, pot.

# Gray Rainbow

We're stuck in 2013, there's no doubt,
you're still alive, and I, your ghost-to-be,
apprenticing. We're stuck historically,
semantically, syntactically, without
a possibility of lighting out.
You've started on the latest therapy,
a miracle of pharmacology.
It takes a new path you're assigned to scout.
You toil through brambles, fend off every threat,
send signals from the wilderness, leave blaze
marks in hard bark. Your fire keeps wolves at bay
a while. You contemplate their rainbow grays,
their gazes, slate to gold to blue. You let
them watch you live. They let us find our way.

# US Patent 6,469, "Buoying Vessels Over Shoals"

Just out of reach is where inventions wait
for most of us. Our sixteenth president
was holder of a patent, but its fate
was swiftly to be judged irrelevant.
A sort of Mae West for a riverboat
in trouble, the device did not take off.
Most inspirations are of lesser note
even than his. They haven't heft enough.
Or they are perfect answers but we fail
to pose the proper questions. Tinkerers
have met a need sometimes. But none avail
except in gross material affairs.
It wasn't thwarted plans to tame a shoal
that rendered Lincoln inconsolable.

# Vaccination

They say they've made a molecule to save
us from the latest plague. We must rejoice
at this while knowing how our spirits crave
catastrophe. We say, in Hamlet's voice,
"The play's the thing." Heroic posturing
convinces in Act Two, but by Act Five?
And even then there's no real reckoning.
How many villains vaccines leave alive.
Unbated swords and poisoned cups and cries
don't rid us of our ghosts. They'll prowl the wall
long past the day or night the last plague dies,
long after the last flag and rampart fall.
I don't believe in ghosts. Our agony
dies when we do. But ghosts believe in me.

# The Clepsydra

The sundial, water clock, and hourglass
agree on time, but time conceals its hand;
one trusts the sun, another, sea, to pass
its strait. The third depends on grains of sand.
To measure time itself, a cheap watchband
does quite as well as any timepiece made,
just on a different scale. Time will expand
or shrink to any length to win your trade.
What gauges time is time: we watch it fade,
it watches us. This isn't quite a sport,
although it feels like childhood games we played.
It's more like hobbies of the rarer sort.
Revive the clepsydra. Raise up Stonehenge,
where time from timelessness exacts revenge.

# A Playbill for Sunset

There's always time to watch a setting sun,
as long as you entrust to metaphor
"there," "always," "time," and "watch" and "set" and "sun."
What else is that technique of thinking for?
The fear and pity Aristotle swore
were "purged" by tragedy, or at least "claimed"
they "were," were metaphorical, but bore
inside themselves the very things they named.
In any case, the western sky's inflamed,
and what you make of that, well, watch and wait.
Just take your time, no need to feel ashamed.
A ghost light lingers if we stay up late.
There's always time. The sun will always set.
In mask and buskins, dusk may answer yet.

# Acknowledgments

Deep thanks to my editor and publisher Steve Semken; to Larry Baker for prompting me to collect the poems in this book and for advocating for it; to Astrid Hilger Bennett for her artwork; and to Joseph Patrick for his drawing and Ben Patrick for permission to include it.

I am grateful to my relations, mentors, teachers, colleagues, and friends for their encouragement and commentary along the way. For their furtherance of poems collected here I offer thanks to Jim Bass, Julie and Wendell Burkey, Maryrose Carroll, Margaret and Jason Castagna, Jeanne Collins and Albert Whetter, Jim Edwards, Joan Fallert and Dan Boliaris, Dan Fick, Lynn Forbing, Terry Jones, Roxanne and Susan Koudelka, Cecile and Ruedi Kuenzli, Heidi and Ron Mace, Nina Metzner, Norm Michaud, Sherri and Harvey Miller, Judy Polumbaum, Lauren Rabinovitz, Mark Reckase, Deborah and Tim Roberts, Ginger Russell, Cameron and Ron Schallawitz, Tracy Schoenle, Cindy and Jim Siergey, Julie Tallman, Mary Kay Temple, Jan Weissmiller, Sandy Whelan, and Barbara and Larry Yerkes.

For their support of my writing, the editors of the publications listed below, in which forty-six of the sixty-seven poems in this book first appeared, have my warmest appreciation.

Previously published:

| | |
|---|---|
| *Able Muse* | The Greystone |
| *After Hours* | Das Boot; Hild |
| *Amethyst Review* | St. Mary's; Little Victories; The Rental; The Lyrebird |
| *Blue Unicorn* | Tornado Sonnet; Green; The Inlet |
| *Common Ground Review* | Fom al-Haut; Wavelength |
| *Ekphrasis* | Found Object; Les Îles de la Grande Jatte |
| *Grand Little Things* | Time's Arrow; New Year's Morning; Neap Tide; Cottonmouth; The Hounds; Stranded; Unfailingly; Vaccination; The Clepsydra |
| *In Situ* | Episode; The Sublime |
| *Indefinite Space* | The Siege |
| *Innisfree Poetry Journal* | The Parrots; US Patent 6,469, "Buoying Vessels Over Shoals" |
| *International Journal of Whole Person Care* | Gray Rainbow |
| *Light* | Ferlinghetti |
| *Lyrical Iowa* | Diving |
| *Measure* | Tomato Vines |
| *Midwest Quarterly* | Belle Epoque; Late May; Practically Speaking; Monarchy; The Aspen; The Scavenger |
| *Plains Poetry Journal* | The Great Pyramid of Des Moines; Out on Route 6 |
| *Poetry &* | Out Back |
| *The Road Not Taken* | The Armadillo; Dispositions |
| *Slant* | Bloodroot; Storm Windows |
| *Wine Cellar Press* | A Playbill for Sunset |

**Dan Campion** was born in 1949 in Oak Park, Illinois, and grew up on the West Side of Chicago, where he attended Francis Scott Key School and Austin High School. He received an AB in English from the University of Chicago in 1970, held several factory jobs, and then worked as an editor for Library Resources, Inc., Encyclopaedia Britannica, and the Follett Publishing Company. He received an MA from the Program for Writers at the University of Illinois at Chicago in 1975. In 1978 he and his life partner JoAnn Castagna moved to Iowa City, Iowa, where both received PhDs in 1989 from the University of Iowa. He served as a visiting assistant professor of English there from 1991 through 1995 and worked from 1984 to 2013 as an editor for the educational company ACT.

*Syncline* magazine published a selection of his poems as a special issue titled *Calypso* in 1981. His study *Peter De Vries and Surrealism*, published by Bucknell University Press in 1995, describes how deeply the avant-garde influenced the Chicago native De Vries, particularly during his years editing *Poetry*. With Jim Perlman and Ed Folsom he edited *Walt Whitman: The Measure of His Song* (1981; 2nd ed. 1998; 3rd ed. 2019). More than eight hundred of his poems have appeared in magazines and anthologies since the mid-1970s. JoAnn was one of his first editors, publishing poems of his in her poetry magazine *Poetry &*, which also served as a newsletter of Chicago poetry events in 1976 through 1978. Since her death in 2013 he has continued to live and write poems in Iowa City, addressing many of those poems to her.

The Ice Cube Press began publishing in 1991 to focus on how to live with the natural world and to better understand how people can best live together in the communities they share and inhabit. Using the literary arts to explore life and experiences in the heartland of the United States we have been recognized by a number of well-known writers including: Bill Bradley, Gary Snyder, Gene Logsdon, Wes Jackson, Patricia Hampl, Greg Brown, Jim Harrison, Annie Dillard, Ken Burns, Roz Chast, Jane Hamilton, Daniel Menaker, Kathleen Norris, Janisse Ray, Craig Lesley, Alison Deming, Harriet Lerner, Richard Lynn Stegner, Richard Rhodes, Michael Pollan, David Abram, David Orr, and Barry Lopez. We've published a number of well-known authors including: Mary Swander, Jim Heynen, Mary Pipher, Bill Holm, Connie Mutel, John T. Price, Carol Bly, Marvin Bell, Debra Marquart, Ted Kooser, Stephanie Mills, Bill McKibben, Craig Lesley, Elizabeth McCracken, Derrick Jensen, Dean Bakopoulos, Rick Bass, Linda Hogan, Pam Houston, Paul Gruchow and Bill Moyers. Check out Ice Cube Press books on our web site, join our email list, Facebook group, or follow us on Twitter. Visit booksellers, museum shops, or any place you can find good books and support our truly honest to goodness independent publishing projects and discover why we continue striving to "hear the other side."

Ice Cube Press, LLC (Est. 1991)
North Liberty, Iowa, Midwest, USA
Resting above the Silurian and Jordan aquifers
steve@icecubepress.com
Check us out on Twitter and Facebook.
www.icecubepress.com

Celebrating Thirty-One Years of Independent Publishing

To Fenna Marie—
A gleaming and radiant
alpenglow of light,
dusk to dawn
day to night